MW01087396

Identity Crisis

Jim Hockaday

ISBN 978 1792697043

Table of Contents

ARE YOU MY MOTHER?

DO YOU REMEMBER the children's book called, *Are You my Mother?* It is a wonderfully written book about a bird that hatches from its egg while the mother is away from the nest. All alone, the bird decides to look for its mother. As it ventures out of the nest, the bird encounters different animals and machines. The bird asks each animal if it is his mother, and each animal replies, "I am not your mother." He also asks each machine if it is his mother, but none of them answer his question. The last machine, an earthmover, scoops up the little bird and puts him back into his nest. Just then, the mother bird returns, and the little bird asks her the question he had asked all of the things he had encountered, "Are you my mother?" The mother bird says, "Yes, I am your mother," which satisfies the little bird forever.

This story perfectly illustrates an identity crisis. The little bird needed to know his mother, so he could understand who he was. He tried to identify with all of the other things he came into contact with, but none of them could relate to him. The human race has been evolving for thousands of years, but we are unconcerned about the direction of our evolution. For the majority of people, the present identity of humanity is not even a consideration. And for those who study societal norms, what pattern of human development would cause researchers to question whether or not humanity is at the correct norm? What is used to determine the norm? These are questions that need to be answered! Just like the bird who strayed from the nest before it understood its origin, how would we know to question the truth of alternative identities when we don't know our own?

Identity Crisis presents God's original design for mankind. With God's purpose clearly defined, could man excel far beyond where he is at present? How exciting would life be if we could live on God's terms, with God's influence and help? Until we have clarity, how can we consider that there is a possibility.

Welcome to *Identity Crisis*.

Chapter 1
In the beginning

I BELIEVE THAT when God created the heavens and the earth, He was making a place suitable for His main creation, *man*. Man would be the center of attention on the earth. He would be God's chosen creation to manage *everything* that God had made.

In *Genesis* 1:23-27, God said that he made every earthly creature "according to its kind." This phrase was repeated many times in these few verses. God emphasized this phrase because it is important for you to know that you were also made according to your kind; that you were made in the image of God. *The Living Bible* does a great job with the translation of verses 26 and 27:

26 "Then God said, "Let us make a man —someone like ourselves, to be the master of all life upon the earth and in the skies and in the seas."

27 So God made man like his Maker. Like God did God make man; Man and maid did he make them" (TLB).

Essentially, God said that just as he had made all other creatures according to their kind; he desired to make a creation after His own kind. In other words, you are created as a God-kind of being. That's why verse 27 says, *"like God did God make man."* Human beings, then, are in the God class, a God-type of being. The *Concordant Translation* says,

27 "And now we will make Human beings; they will be like US, and resemble US."

What do you think about being made just like God? Does it stir your curiosity to know there is more to you than you might realize? Is it possible that you have the ability *to bring things into existence* like God did? If so, what changes in yourself would you make if you could?

God had the perfect opportunity to create someone like himself and he seized it! Imagine that you could create a perfect substitute for yourself that could handle all of your affairs. What if the substitute was so equally created that he or she could perform the tasks you would do, as well as you would do them?

If you owned a business, and it was thriving, making it necessary to add employees, who would you want to hire? How could you find someone that could flawlessly complete a specific task the way you do, or someone that would care about the success of the business the way you do? You would have a difficult time finding someone just like you. But what if you could "duplicate" yourself? Wouldn't that solve all of your problems? You see, God had no group of earthly be-ings to choose from. Everything he was creating was brand new . . . the perfect opportunity! He could create exactly what he wanted. If you were creating someone to take over your job; who or what would you create? Obviously, someone just like you!! God multiplied his effectiveness. Now, while God is doing what he needs to do, he is still running the planet through you. God called this marvelous invention, "man".

The actual creation process of man was unique. Genesis 2:7 shows us what God did to create man. First, he formed him out of the dust of the ground. God made a physical body composed of dust and capable of living in this earthly world. Sickness, disease, and death were not part of this original creation. God made the human body to live forever. God made man perfect!

Let's look again at Genesis 2:7,

"And the LORD God formed man of the dust of the ground, and breathed into his nostrils the breath of life; and man became a living being" (NKJV).

I've always enjoyed looking at things from a different perspective. Can you see how God's perfectly formed body for man was completely receptive to the

life that God breathed into him? This is very important for you to see. The life and nature of God is a perfect fit for the body of man. It was this life that was to sustain the physical body. All compartments of man, his spirit, soul and body were to complement each other.

The "breath of God" breathed into the body of man, made man a spirit. Man became a "living being" because of this breath.

It was not until God breathed into man that he was identified as a "living being." His heart was comprised of his spirit and soul. The spirit of man is a spiritual being, the "real" person. The soul, which is the will, intellect, and emotions of man is the second part of man which learns from and can be influenced by either the spirit or body. The spirit and soul were in harmony together as they lived in a human body.

The original design of man was as follows: the *spirit* is the real person; the *soul* is to gain knowledge from and complement the spirit; the *body* which connects man to this earthly world is to remain submissive to the spirit and soul. If you remember, man didn't pay attention to his body until after he sinned. This should help you to see that the body was not the "central focus" of man. To the contrary, the spirit of man was in direct fellowship with God. The soul responded in all its capacity from a spiritually perfect understanding. The body was doing what it was created for: facilitating the intentions of the spirit while connected to the physical world. The harmony of man's spirit, soul and body is "God's" original intention for man. Man had been made in the physical and spiritual likeness of the Eternal God; he is the exact manifestation and representation of God.

Jesus was and is the exact expression of the Eternal God, his Father. Jesus proved these truths are so. In Luke chapter 9 Jesus took his disciples, Peter, James, and John up the mountain to pray. As he prayed, his face began to "alter in appearance" and the clothes he was wearing began to glisten with the glory of God. What actually happened here was the glory or life of God that lived on the inside of Jesus began to manifest itself through the body of Jesus and extended itself right through his clothes. This couldn't have happened if the soul of Jesus wasn't open and receptive to the spiritual world. This means it is possible for the presence of God to be worn like a garment. The psalmist talks about the "garment of praise" being worn instead of the "spirit of heaviness." Paul talks further about our mortality being swallowed up by God's immortality. He describes it by mentioning in second Corinthians chapter 5 that he desires to be further clothed with heavenly clothing. This is the same glory that was so evident in the life of Jesus and was apparent on the Mount of Transfiguration.

How amazing it is that God **made** us and **fashioned** us for his glory. What an awesome privilege it is to be made so much like God that we can wear his glory, and fellowship with his Spirit, in the same manner as Jesus himself. This is something we need to comprehend and accept in our spirits.

Chapter 2
In His Image

THE FIRST THING that God did after he formed man and breathed the breath of life into him was to bestow upon him the dominion that God himself walks in. Dominion is the authority of God, that is built into the life and nature of God. In Genesis 1:26 God said,

*"Let Us [Father, Son, and Holy Spirit] make mankind in Our image, after Our likeness, and **let them have complete authority** over the fish of the sea, the birds of the air, the [tame] beasts, and over all of the earth, and over everything that creeps upon the earth"* (AMP).

There is a principle revealed in this verse that must be understood; you will always find that dominion will automatically follow a revelation of the position that God has created you for. When God made man as Himself, dominion was a natural addition to man. Dominion comes with **being made** in the image of God.

Using this dominion is a natural process as we discover the truth of our place in Christ. When you know that you are healed because of the "finished work of Jesus," the authority to drive sickness out of your body will rise up in you naturally. Dominion is a by-product of our position with God.

Likewise, when you find out that Jesus became poor so that we through his poverty might be made rich, then you will automatically sense the authority to change your present place of lack. Naturally, you will rise up to say and do something about your situation when you know you no longer need to accept it.

Are you starting to see your true identity?? God gave man complete authority over everything that he made. I don't think anyone would disagree that man is the most intelligent life form upon the earth. However, it might be difficult for most folks to swallow the fact that God turned the control and rule of the earth over to man. This means that God is not *first-in-charge* when it comes to

this planet. He believes that he successfully made a more than capable replace-
ment to handle the responsibilities of the
earth.

Man has the responsibility of allowing or restraining all spiritual influences
in the earth. According to God's will, man
can enjoy fellowship from God and
thereby release his influence upon the
earth, which would be the intention God
had in mind. Or, man can reject God and
refuse to walk in his intended authority.

Deuteronomy 30:19-20 will help us
to imagine the power of our authority.

*19 "This day I call heaven and earth as
witnesses against you that I have set before you life and death, blessings and
curses. Now choose life, so that you and
your children may live,"*
*20 "and that you may love the LORD
your God, listen to his voice, and hold
fast to him. For the LORD is your life,
and he will give you many years in the*

land he swore to give to your fathers,
Abraham, Isaac and Jacob," (NIV).

Can you see that life and death, blessings and curses have no power of choice? These things are in the earth, yet they have no influence until a human being accepts them. We would equate life and blessings to God and His goodness. The choice is not with life or death, it's with us. Jesus made the statement in John chapter 10:18 that he had "the power to lay his life down and take it up," he went on to say that, "no man can take my life - I must lay it down of my own accord." It was in the decision of the Lord whether he would die or not. Remember the struggle in the garden of Gethsemane? Jesus was torn between God's will and the power to choose. He ultimately chose to lay his life down and become the "sacrificial lamb" for humanity. He said three times, "Not my will, but thy will be done." He did, however, struggle to do so.

There are many interesting incidents in the Word of God that support these thoughts. Take for instance the conversation that Moses and God had concerning the children of Israel. In Numbers 14 we read how, after the law was given, the children of Israel were complaining against God in the wilderness. The Lord spoke to Moses and voiced his right to exercise judgment against the sin of the Israelites. Moses interceded and pled the case, like a lawyer would do, to obtain God's mercy for the people. He reminded God that it would not be right to destroy the children of Israel, because the world would hear about it and say that God was able to deliver the children of Israel from Egyptian bondage but unable to bring them into the promised land. God responded by withholding his judgment.

For a moment, let's see things from God's perspective. He created man for fellowship. It would not be his nature to create and then destroy. God loves His creation and he desires to bring complete and final redemption to all. However, because God designed the very structure of authority, with man having the right to govern, he must work with and through man to openly satisfy his will. If you see this correctly then you will also understand why the Lord was pleased to pardon the children of Israel. With man's cooperation God can bring about his purpose.

Ultimately, God desired mercy for the children of Israel. Mercy was granted at this time because Moses assumed the role of mediator. In Ezekiel 22:30-23:1, we see another good example of the divine position that God placed man in. Notice how God sought for someone to exercise authority, on the earth, for the sin that called for God's judgment.

30 "And I sought for a man among them, that should make up the hedge, and stand in the gap before me for the land, that I should not destroy it: but I found none."
31 Therefore have I poured out mine indignation upon them; I have consumed them with the fire of my wrath: their own way have I recompensed upon their heads, saith the Lord GOD" (KJV).

You may ask, "Why doesn't God just do what he wants?" If God could, we would all be going into the "millennium" tomorrow. Fortunately for mankind, because man was created to be the one in authority, he is the one in charge and the one who will ultimately become a conduit for God's grace, or a barrier to that grace. Since God could not find anyone to stand in the gap for the sin of the people during the time of Ezekiel, judgment was served. Notice in verse 31 that the recompense was upon their own heads according to the choices they made.

Thank God Jesus stood in the gap for all of us at Calvary. God is just and desires mercy; this is the reason that Jesus became the *mercy seat* of all the judgment for the whole earth. This is the **gospel message**, the sin problem has been solved through the death, burial and resurrection of our Lord. In the New Covenant God placed all our sin upon Jesus, removing the penalty and punishment for sin. However, under the Old

Covenant we know that when sin pro-
voked God, he was required to bring
judgment.

I trust that you are seeing the importance of the subject—the authority of
man. Every individual will make choices
that define his or her life. Neither God
nor the devil can make you do anything,
so you must choose to walk with God
and follow his amazing plan for your life.

Chapter 3
The Dominion of Man

IN GENESIS chapter two God gave man two commands. The first command was **not to eat** of the tree of the knowledge of good and evil, and the second command was to **guard** the garden. It would be important for man to obey these commands, for they would significantly affect his quality of life.

If we will recall how God put man in charge of running the earth, then the next sequence of events makes perfect sense. Adam's instructions were simple: to guard the garden and to refrain from eating from the tree of the knowledge of good and evil. You would assume that if you were told to guard the garden, there might possibly be an intruder to be on the lookout for.

The Word declares that Satan is subtle and crafty. He will never allow us to see him as he really is. We know from the prophet Isaiah, who saw into the future at the throne of God, that one day we will see Satan for who he is. Isaiah reveals that our response will be "astonishment" as we see Satan in such a defeated form. The words that Isaiah records are, *Is this what caused nations to tremble and brought men to their knees?"* Let us on purpose never allow Satan or his deceptions to cause us to fear or draw back from our bold position as children of the Most High God. We always have the upper hand and with God on our side who can be against us?

Satan very cunningly questioned Eve about what God said and whether God would do what he said. Be ever so careful when you begin to question the truthfulness of what God has said to you and whether he will do what he said. This is a place of deception, a trap set by the enemy, to move you from your strong position of faith and determination to a weak, unsettled position of doubt and fear.

Genesis 3:1-6,

1 Now the serpent was more crafty than any of the wild animals the LORD God had made. He said to the woman, "Did God really say, 'You must not eat from any tree in the garden'?"
2 The woman said to the serpent, 'We may eat fruit from the trees in the garden,'
3 "but God did say, 'You must not eat fruit from the tree that is in the middle of the garden, and you must not touch it, or you will die.'"
4 "You will not surely die," the serpent said to the woman."
5 "For God knows that when you eat of it your eyes will be opened, and you will be like God, knowing good and evil."
6 "When the woman saw that the fruit of the tree was good for food and pleasing to the eye, and also desirable for gaining wisdom, she took some and ate it. She also gave some to her husband, who was with her, and he ate it" (NIV).

Notice that Satan's temptation began with questions. First, he questioned what God said. This is the reason God made his word infallible, so you will never have to question what he has said. If "it's written" then it is more stable than the earth itself. Next, Satan urged Eve to consider that what God had said would **not** happen. Here, Satan questions the faithfulness and integrity of God. These attributes of God that cause such great faith in the hearts of those who follow the Lord are being questioned. As Eve begins to doubt God's word, Satan further piques her curiosity by suggesting that if she eats of the tree she will be like God. But Eve was already like God! In the first chapter of Genesis, the Bible says that God created man in His image and likeness.

This was the very reason the Jews sought to stone Jesus. They said that he *being a man* was trying to make himself God. Jesus didn't make himself God, God made him God. God the Father **made** the humanity of Jesus, the Son of God. Jesus was just living out of the makeup or substance of His being.

Satan is the one who longs to be like God. However, this will never happen because God made angels as created beings in a class lower than man and God. Satan is a fallen angel. Do you see now how important it is to **know** who you are and how God has made you? Satan will always steer you away from considering or seeing the full picture of who you are. Satan cannot stop you from being the person God made you to be, but he will try to keep you from knowing it. He will always lower your expectations and place your thoughts on the insecurity of the flesh rather than allowing you to remain in a consciousness of strength and faith.

When Eve sinned, she was deceived; however, when Adam sinned, he willfully took of the fruit. In his disobedience, he delivered his place of authority on the earth to a new "master," Satan. Our authority lies in whom we give our allegiance. Once Adam sinned, authority was given or transferred to Satan. God told Adam that if he ate of the tree he was commanded not to eat of, that he would surely die. God wasn't talking about physical death initially but spiritual death. This is the reason why man is doomed to a life of sin, because his nature has changed from the nature of God to the nature of the devil. Man's heart became corrupted through sin and thus his nature or spirit became sinful. Remember, God created everything to reproduce after its own kind. An animal will reproduce after its own kind because it is in the nature of the animal to do so. So, also a man will reproduce after his own kind. As a result of Adam and Eve's change in allegiance, now all men are made sinful, according to Romans 5:12.

"Therefore, as sin came into the world through one man, and death as the result of sin, so death spread to all men, [no one being able to stop it or to escape its power] because all men sinned" (Romans 5:12 AMPC).

The creation that God had made was clean and filled with life. Now that sin has entered the world, all men are filled with the nature of sin and death. Man is no longer in fellowship with God.

I Corinthians 15:21-22 says,

"Death happens to people because of what one man (Adam) did, but the rising from death also happened because of one man — Christ. For just as all die the spiritual death in common with Adam, so all will return to spiritual life in common with Christ" (DEAF Translation).

Notice the phrase, "die the spiritual death". This phrase reveals the essence of sin. The wrong action of Adam affected the spiritual nature of man. Once made in the image of God, now man is destined to exist through the sin nature of Satan. This change is permanent unless spiritual redemption is possible. From the beginning God established that everything would reproduce after its own kind, meaning that sinful man will forever give birth to sin-natured beings. First Corinthians 15:21-22 says that man would only find hope in a savior; someone who could bypass the sinful nature of man and legally defeat the power of sin held by Satan.

The ramifications of sin, within the heart of man, would do even greater damage than the initial shock of eternal separation from God. The sinful nature of Satan would also bring with it the attributes of sin that have become "second nature" to the world. Fear and hatred are synonymous with the power of sin, along with every other hideous insecurity and rebellion. The effect of sin has proven fatal through the centuries with war, famine, disease and sickness, hatred, and the brutal treatment of mankind. All these and more are the natural responses from the heart of a sin-natured human being.

Ephesians 2:1-3,
1 "As for you, you were dead in your transgressions and sins,"
2 "in which you used to live when you followed the ways of this world and of the ruler of the kingdom of the air, the spirit who is now at work in those who are disobedient."
3 "All of us also lived among them at one time, gratifying the cravings of our sinful nature and following its desires and

thoughts. Like the rest, we were by na-
ture objects of wrath" (NIV).

It becomes very easy to see why there is no hope in the world without a savior. Every other religion deals only with the psychological efforts of man to improve his behavior. Some have ac-cessed the spiritual world to find enlight-enment, yet there is still no hope without a savior. No other religion has a savior who has crossed over the barrier of the nature of sin and returned a champion, victorious over its eternal penalty called death, hell and the grave.

Before we begin to talk about our *substitute* and his finished work to de-stroy the works of the devil, I want you to see something awesomely important to the eternal dominion of man and the demise of the devil. In Genesis 4:3-7,

4 "But Abel brought fat portions from some of the firstborn of his flock. The LORD looked with favor on Abel and his offering,"

5 *"but on Cain and his offering he did not look with favor. So Cain was very angry, and his face was downcast."*
6 *"Then the LORD said to Cain, 'Why are you angry? Why is your face downcast?*
7 *If you do what is right, will you not be accepted? But if you do not do what is right, sin is crouching at your door; it desires to have you, but you must master it'"* (NIV).

The word "master" is the same word for dominion found in the 26th verse of Genesis chapter one. God was specifically telling a man "born in sin" to master or take dominion over sin. Remember, Cain was contemplating murdering his brother, Abel. Not only was God against what Cain was planning, he went as far as to give Cain instruction on how to avoid this evil impulse. Does this mean that sinful man has a "measure" of authority? The answer is a resounding "yes". Although the heart is sinful by nature, the decisions of man are still according to "free" choice. The reason behind this measure of authority is found in the "structure of authority" that God established in our rank and position, as creatures created by God.

First, we know that God the Father, God the Son and God the Holy Spirit, the divine Trinity are the source of all life without question. God's name from the beginning was *Elohim*, the One and only true God. There are not thousands of gods as some religions believe. **God is God and there is no other.** Think for a moment how we make other religions look attractive by our lack of initiative. Without the trademarks of Christianity; the signs, wonders and answers to prayers, our understanding of God looks extremely weak. This lack of tangible results gives one the idea that our concept of God just barely surpasses the gods of all the other religions. Every other form of religion comes from the lies and deceptions of Satan himself. He has taken many good thoughts and twisted them until other religions look very similar to Christianity. Let us never forget that Satan is lower than man on the "totem pole" of life. He is not, and never will be, in the class of God.

When God made angels, He made them as "beings" unto themselves. They have their own identity and they have a tremendous place of assistance in the plan of God. The function of their existence seems to evolve around fulfilling the plan of God. From the beginning of the Scriptures we see angels giving their assistance to God as help to mankind. We know that there are angels who seem to have their assignment in heaven. They worship and give continual praise to God and Jesus the Son. They provide a tremendous support in the overall operation of heaven. However, when we see them in operation on the earth, they are giving assistance to man. Angels are ministering spirits sent to bring aid to the "heirs of promise." We are those heirs.

Satan, in his heyday, was at best a servant to God and to man. Jesus told his disciples that he saw Satan fall like "lightening" to the earth. In other words, there was a big puff of smoke and the best that Satan ever was, was taken from him. He was reduced to a spiritual entity without purpose.

I will explain Satan's demise and man's authority so you can correctly envision the victory of the Lord Jesus Christ. John G. Lake, a man used mightily in divine healing at the turn of the last century was quoted as saying, "No Christian will experience the victory of our Lord Jesus Christ until he recognizes that the enemy is a completely vanquished foe."

In the next chapter, we will see why legally only one man has ever qualified as a redeemer.

Chapter 4
What choice will you make?

WHAT WOULD QUALIFY A MAN to redeem the world from the nature of sin? Is it possible that a man could exist without the nature of sin? How could one be born a human without going through the sin-nature process? Remember, when sin-natured parents give birth, that same sin nature is transferred to the child. So, how could a man qualify to redeem the world from the nature of sin?

Throughout the centuries man's sin has continued to spiral out of control. There is literally no possibility of man redeeming man if all men have sinned and fallen short of the glory of God. The redeemer, that all the earth beckons, is someone not tainted by sin. God certainly is not limited; he actually had a plan before the world was.

1 John 4:1-3,

2 *"This is how you can recognize the Spirit of God: Every spirit that acknowledges that Jesus Christ has come in the flesh is from God,"*
3 *"but every spirit that does not acknowledge Jesus is not from God. This is the spirit of the antichrist, which you have heard is coming and even now is already in the world"* (NIV).

Why is it so important for us to acknowledge that Jesus Christ has come in the flesh? To acknowledge this is to ascertain that Jesus was indeed a man. Without the humanity of Jesus being revealed to mankind, we would be unaware of our purpose and the ultimate intent of God the Father. Even Jesus emphasized and, you could even say, over emphasized the fact that he was human. More than ninety times in the gospels, Jesus refers to himself as the Son of Man . . . a phrase used to authenticate his humanity. Here is the important fact to the humanity of Jesus: the only possible way for redemption to legally hold up in a court of law, spiritually, is for a man to purchase back what the first man Adam lost. Satan understood from the prophetic word God spoke to him in the Garden of Eden that the "Seed" of the woman would crush the head of the serpent. Notice that the woman, being human, would have a seed which would be human as well. The "law of Genesis" is at work here. Everything God made, including man, would produce after *its own kind*. Sin-natured man could only produce sin-natured offspring. Satan was not aware of God's secret and illustrious plan to redeem man. Therefore, Satan walked right into his own destruction and an eternal death warrant.

"Instead, we continually speak of this wonderful wisdom that comes from God, hidden before now in a mystery. It is his secret plan, destined before the ages, to bring us into glory. None of the rulers of this present world order understood it, for if they had, they never would have crucified the Lord of shining glory" (1 Corinthians 2:7-8 (TPT).

God's secret wisdom was the plan that brought His Son into the earth, disguised in an "earth suit," living as a man. Through His death, burial and resurrection, Jesus would make provision for the whole world to experience a new birth. All this began through the "virgin birth."

God found a woman pure of heart and flesh: a virgin named Mary. She was the perfect candidate for the miracle birth of Jesus. God sent His angel to announce to Mary that she was chosen to be the mother of the Son of God. Mary provided the womb for the Seed of God's word to develop. By the power of the Holy Spirit, the Son of God was conceived. Jesus was born without the sin nature that had proven fatal throughout the history of man. The heart and blood of Jesus was as pure as the heart of God. Not since the beginning of all things, with Adam, had there been a man **filled** with the nature of God. This eternal nature enabled him while in the form of man, to represent His Father to the world.

Philippians 2:5-8,

5 "Your attitude should be the same as that of Christ Jesus:"
6 "Who, being in very nature God, did not consider equality with God something to be grasped,"
7 "but made himself nothing, taking the very nature of a servant, being made in human likeness."
8 "And being found in appearance as a man" (NIV).

We have looked at this passage as a lesson in humility, and so it is. In "light" of our subject, however, let's first look at the details of this humility. Remember, we are discovering the reason that Jesus was the perfect mediator and stand-in for the world. Verse 5 declares that our attitude should be the same as Jesus. You could say that it is important to think like Jesus, or see one self like He sees Himself.

Verses 6-8, at face value, help us to see the humanity of Jesus. While his nature and the essence of his being was God, he took on flesh and became a man. This in part had much to do with his humility. He was perfect in spirit; no other man could say this. At the same time he was "man in flesh," he is "God in spirit."

Traditionally, we look at verse 7 and see that Jesus, in his humility, was **made** a servant. This has fed our insecurities throughout the ages as Christians have accepted our miserable fate—that we as humans are doomed to lowliness. If you were to consider that when God made man he did so in his image and his likeness, it would be difficult to conclude that humanity is equal to lowliness. After all, even now there is a human, or man, seated at the right hand of God. His name is Jesus!

We have accepted such a low view of humanity over the years that we tend to gravitate to the worst possible thought. This is something that Jesus did not do. He did not apologize for being human. At no time did he leave the impression that, because he was human, he could not express the reality of his Father God. Paul said in Hebrews 1:3 that

Jesus was the "divine expression of God in flesh." In John 14:11, Jesus said that you could get an accurate image of the Father by looking closely at him; "If you've seen me, you've seen the Father." Jesus leads us to believe that his humanity did not impair or hinder his ability to reveal, in full, the heart and likeness of the Father. Wow!

"Let this mind be in you which was also in Christ Jesus, 6 who, being in the form of God, did not consider it robbery to be equal with God, 7 but made Himself of no reputation, taking the form of a bondservant, and coming in the likeness of men" Philippines 2:5-7 (NKJV).

Here we see that Jesus considered being equal with God was not an offense to God. As a man, Jesus considered himself equal with God! Before Jesus was born in the Earth, he had to empty himself of his godly privileges. As a man, this did not hinder Jesus from fully representing the Father. To be **equal with** God simply means: to represent Him. To be **equal to** God would be to replace

God. Mankind can never replace God, nor would we want to; however, we can "represent" God. To do so explains why we are fearfully and wonderfully made!

This is the reason why, "being a servant" makes so much sense. If your concept of "servanthood" is to live life without any authority; to do only what you are told by those who hold you in bondage, then your perception is incorrect. From the perspective of Jesus, he was serving others because he had something to **give**. When you understand that as a representative you have the ability of the one you represent, then you will release this ability to others.

The mind of Jesus understood who he was and what he had come to this earth to do. Yes, he was *human* and this was positive. No, he didn't have the full potential and glory that he had before he came; however, the divine nature of God, living in the human body of Jesus, was more than enough to express God to the earth (John 17:5). Jesus did have complete access to an unlimited supply of whatever he needed to accomplish his mission (John 3:34). As a result, Jesus went about doing good and healing those in need. Our attitude in life should be one of servanthood; learning how to appreciate and honor others above ourselves. As a result of our position in Christ, we have the privilege even as Jesus did of serving and loving others with the same ability of God.

Jesus was humble. This means, first, he was respectful of the heart and desires of the One he was submitted to. He came to do the will of his Father. Second, it means he was willing to see the needs of others as a service that he had come to fulfill.

I trust you are seeing why Jesus was the only human on the earth capable of fulfilling the assignment to redeem the world. The humility of Jesus, which was his strength, was the reason why he continued with each moment to embrace the heart and will of his Father. His humility kept him mission minded. He never varied from his purpose. His life was absorbed in fulfilling the will of the Father, which meant destroying the works of the devil, thereby releasing mankind to experience the "Love of God."

Chapter 5
Only One Way to Fix the Problem

CHAPTER FOUR was such an important chapter . . . we learned that we too can have the mind of Christ. Jesus was heavily persecuted for considering himself to be God's Son. Seeing himself one with God is really the reason why the Pharisees put Jesus on the cross. This attitude against the "deity" of Christ is a direct assault from Satan. He detests the idea that Jesus is the Christ, anointed and appointed as the *Savior* of the world.

When Jesus prayed for all believers (John 17), he prayed that we would understand that just as he is one with the Father, so are we one with him. He prayed that nothing would hinder this unity. This is the reason why Satan fights so relentlessly against those who believe. He wants us to remain ignorant concerning our position and privileges as sons of God.

Identification encompasses the "secret" to our victory and boldness in life. *Identification* means: to be identical; to be in the same condition; to make one and the same; equal in every respect; to consider as one; sameness; having the same source.

As you can see, you would need at least two people, or things, involved for identification work. Romans 5:12, 15, and 19 show us that two men represented, and affected, the whole human race.

12 "Therefore, as sin came into the world through one man, and death as the result of sin, so death spread to all men, [no one being able to stop it or to escape its power] because all men sinned,"

17 "For if because of one man's trespass (lapse, offense) death reigned through that one, much more surely will those who receive [God's] overflowing grace (unmerited favor) and the free gift of righteousness [putting them into right standing with Himself] reign as kings in

*life through the one Man Jesus Christ
(the Messiah, the Anointed one)."*

*19 "For just as by one man's disobedi-
ence (failing to hear, heedlessness, and
carelessness) the many were constituted
sinners, so by one Man's obedience the
many will be constituted righteous (made
acceptable to God, brought into right
standing with Him)"* (AMP).

If identification is being one and
the same, then all creation, first and
foremost, has identified with Adam and
his sin. Therefore, it was necessary for
Jesus to come to the earth. Through his
perfection, he fulfilled all of the legal
demands against us, and he redeemed
man. Now, it's God's will that all men
identify themselves with Jesus and his
resurrection.

There is something that we must
grasp to understand identification. We
need to know that Jesus became totally
one with fallen man and the new "creation" man became totally one with Jesus. Identification says that Jesus was

made one with man's sin in the same degree as fallen man, and we are made one with God's eternal life in the same degree as the resurrected and glorified Christ.

There was a reason why we spent time in the last chapter describing the humanity of Jesus. Redemption, which is the purchasing back of fallen or sinful man from the clutches of Satan, must be accomplished on legal grounds. Without the legalities and the high courts of heaven being satisfied, the work would not suffice. We certainly would not want Satan to have a viable argument against the child of God. The good news is that Jesus was the perfect sacrifice for the complete purchase of mankind from the "never ending" condition of sin. Along with the humanity of Jesus comes the potential for full pardon. Ultimately, God would first use Jesus to reinstate man to the proper place he had before Adam's high treason, and then he would elevate man's dominion to rule and reign with Christ.

Now, let's understand how identification affects the whole of humanity:

Identification with Adam

• Adam's sin extended to the whole hu-
man race.
• Adam made all unrighteous—unholy.
• You were born under Adam's inheri-
tance (spiritual death).
• You were born under Satan's dominion.
Death passed to all men: no one could
escape.

Identification with Christ.

• Jesus Christ reversed, in born-again
man, what Satan had done through
Adam.
• Jesus made all born-again men right-
eous.
• Jesus imparted to born-again man His
nature—the Divine life he and the Father
have.
• Jesus made us to have sonship with the
Father.
• Jesus delivered us from Satan's domin-
ion.

Before we fully understand how we "identify" with the risen Christ, we must first see how he identifies with fallen man. Jesus came with purpose as the "Lamb of God" to take away the sin of the world. God used a spotless lamb, under the old system of law, to atone for the sin of the people. To *atone* means to cover. The sin of the people was only covered by the sacrifice of a lamb. However, the consciousness of sin continued because there was no deliverance for the sin condition of the people. Their hearts were still sinful by nature. The condition of sin could only be dealt with if the sin nature could be completely altered and made right. In the same way, in the old covenant, the lamb was the sacrificial substitute for the sin of the people. Jesus laid down his life as our "substitute." Instead of YOU paying for your sin, Jesus paid for it. The penalty for sin is death and for this reason Jesus died for us.

Colossians 2:14 says, in the Laubach translation, *"God crossed out the whole debt against us in His account books. He no longer counted the laws that we had broken. He nailed the account book to the cross and closed the account."*

The *New English Bible* translation says, in 2 Corinthians 5:21, *"God made him one with the sinfulness of men…."*

Jesus took our sin and became one with it, so he could identify himself with fallen man. Even though Jesus had never sinned, Jesus willingly paid the penalty for the nature of sin, which was death. There was no getting around the fact that Jesus had to become one with man's sin and die as a sinner even though he had not sinned himself. Paul helps us further understand the gravity of this selfless act in 1 Timothy 3:16, *"And without controversy great is the mystery of godliness: God was manifested in the flesh,* **Justified in the Spirit***, seen by angels, preached among the Gentiles, believed on in the world, received up in glory"* (NKJV).

Notice that you would not have to be justified, which means to be declared righteous in the spirit, unless your spiritual condition was no longer right. Why would God make your spirit perfect and right unless your spirit required it for fellowship? Second Corinthians 5:19 says that God was in Christ, reconciling the world unto Himself. This means He was restoring his fellowship with the world, the spiritual solution for turning enemies into friends. The only way this could be done, when the world continued to express the nature of sin, was for our substitute (Jesus) to be justified in spirit on our behalf.

We know that Jesus was not raised from the dead until **all** humanity was cleared from **all** sin. *Romans 4:25 says, "Who was betrayed and put to death because of our misdeeds and was raised to secure our justification (our acquittal), [making our account balance and absolving us from all guilt before God]." AMPC.* If Jesus was the first born among many brothers, then he went through the transformation process that also makes us righteous.

Jesus died and went to hell to pay the penalty of sin. He went there having become one with the sin nature of sinful man. In order to restore man, he had to taste death and suffer the affliction of sin. Jesus entered hell as a victim and exited hell as the "eternal champion." A man defeated death, hell and the grave. Hebrews 2:14 says, in the *Living Bible*, *"For only as a human being could he die and in dying break the power of the devil."* As we have discussed, you can clearly see how Jesus identified with fallen man. Next, we will see how man identifies with the risen victorious Christ.

Chapter 6
Jesus is the Redeemer

LET'S REVIEW FOR A MOMENT: God
made man in his image and likeness.
This means we were God's perfect solution for his delegation of authority over
the earth, as his created being. When
man sinned, he lost this position of authority with God and became a servant
to his own sin-cursed nature. Sin-natured beings no longer had true fellowship with God, and their eternal future
was doomed to complete separation from
God in a devil's hell. Satan was the father of this race of beings. Man, however,
has a free will and can choose to do good
or to do evil based on his knowledge.
This is the reason that Satan works so
tirelessly to pervert the mind of man. He
wants man's life to be carnal and worldly.
With man being truly subservient to the
flesh and the world, he has very little
chance of seeing the truth of his authority.

The only hope for man in this condition, is a complete rebirth of his spiritual condition. There is no work on the part of man that merits any spiritual advancement. Man is eternally and hopelessly lost without divine intervention from God. Every human being must come to see why they have need of a savior. If man doesn't understand his spiritual condition and his inability to change his sinful self, he will have difficulty reaching out for help. This can only come from a loving God with a plan of salvation that comes through the One, Jesus Christ.

In the same degree that Jesus represented fallen man, by descending into hell's clutches, he also ascended from hell as man's savior and champion over everything representing death, hell and the grave. This is where the church is privileged to experience the legal side of our redemption through "identification" with Christ.

Yes it is true, when Jesus died, we died. Even Colossians 2:20, in the Wuest

Translation says, "*...in view of the fact that you died **with** Christ...;*" Here, the word "with" is used as a preposition. When used in this way, the word "with" means two or more persons or things are together. It also means, because of, at the time of, as completely as, counted with, or into. So, using these definitions we could say we died at the time of Christ; we died as completely as Christ; or we died counted with Christ. Romans 6:8, in the 20th Century Translation says, "*You have shared Christ's death.*" The old man is gone, dead and buried. There is nothing left of him, you are no longer in connection with that old man; you are now connected to God. Thank God Jesus didn't stay dead, and neither did we! We identified with him in his death, so we also get to identify with him in his victory over Satan through his res- urrection.

As Jesus absorbed the burden of the sin of the world, he lay captive to hell's torment. After seeing the brutality in men tormented by Satan, you can imagine the suffering that Jesus endured. For three days he endured hell and the grave on our behalf. He was paying the penalty and punishment for the **nature of sin** that consumed every man and woman past, present or future. Jesus paid for them **all**, every sin that mankind could or would ever commit. Once the demand for justice was served, on the third day life was breathed into him and he came alive! Did you know that Satan remembers this? I Corinthians 2:8 says that if the rulers of the world knew what they were doing when they crucified the Lord of Glory, they never would have done it.

First Peter 3:18 says Jesus was, *"Made alive in His spirit",* Beck Translation. In 1 Timothy 3:16, Paul said that Jesus was "Justified in the Spirit." He was "declared" righteous or made pure in spirit. When this happened, Jesus stood up. He was no longer under the influence of our sin. SIN had been successfully paid for! From this moment, there was no longer a sin problem. Do you remember what Jesus said before he went to the cross? He said that the *tempter* was coming, but he had nothing **on him.** Jesus also told his disciples that no man could take his life. This is why he told Pilate, "You have no authority unless it has been given from above." Jesus walked in absolute dominion.

The restoration of this dominion came at the "transition" from spiritual death to spiritual life. The Knox Translation of Colossians 2:13 says, *"And in giving life to Him, He gave life to you, too, when you lay dead in your sins…."* It was at this point that all hell trembled. The "great" power of God made Jesus alive and filled him with the glory of the eternities. Right here, **Jesus was made the eternal authority of heaven and earth.** Satan, evil spirits, demons, principalities, powers, and hell itself, were no match for the Christ of God. Hebrews 2:14 says that Jesus dethroned the *lord of death*, the devil. The way he did this is described in Colossians 2:15. The Phillips Translation says, *"And then, having drawn the sting of all the powers raged against us he exposed them, shattered,* empty, and defeated, in his final glorious triumphant act!"

Carpenter Translation says, "...and having frisked the top brass and the power boys, and made them prisoners of war, he publicly exposed them." Wand Translation says, "he stripped away like a cast-off garment every demonic rule and authority and made a public exhibition of them...." Jesus so thoroughly defeated Satan, and all of hell, that there is absolutely no fear that will ever hinder man or the plan of God.

Remember, before Jesus died he prayed that nothing would hinder the fact that we are one with him as he is one with God. It's over!! There is nothing left for Jesus to do that will make a difference in the way the earth functions. Roman 8:33-39 tells us that Jesus made us more than conquerors of everything in the realm of spiritual death.

35 "Who shall ever separate us from Christ's love? Shall suffering and affliction and tribulation? Or calamity and dis-

*tress? Or persecution or hunger or desti-
tution or peril or sword?"*
*36 Even as it is written, 'For Thy sake we
are put to death all the day long; we are
regarded and counted as sheep for the
slaughter'" (Psalm 44:22).*
*37 "Yet amid all these things we are
more than conquerors and gain a sur-
passing victory through Him Who loved
us."*
*38 "For I am persuaded beyond doubt
(am sure) that neither death nor life, nor
angels nor principalities, nor things im-
pending and threatening nor things to
come, nor powers,"*
*39 "Nor height nor depth, nor anything
else in all creation will be able to separate us from the love of God which is in
Christ Jesus our Lord"*
(AMP).

This incredible change in Jesus, as
he rose from the dead and was restored
to full privilege as the Son of God, is the
same change that occurs in us at the
moment of our confession and accep-
tance of Jesus as the Lord of our lives.
We then become sons of God. Paul calls

it "becoming a new creation." **It is the finished work of identification.** Not only did Jesus identify with our sinfulness, we identify with his righteousness. Second Corinthians 5:17 in the Translators Translation says, *"If a man is in Christ, there is a new act of creation. The old has gone, the new has come."* Stanley Translation says, *"If anyone has entered into fellowship with Christ, a new world has at once opened unto him, and the old world has passed away."* Isaacs Translation says, *"…to be Christ's man you see, is to be a creature of a new order."*

Ephesians 2:15, in the AMP, says, *"By abolishing in his own crucified flesh the enmity caused by the law with its decrees and ordinances which he annulled; that he from the two might create in himself one new man – one new quality of humanity out of the two making peace."* NL Translation says, *"Then he made of the two peoples one new kind of people like himself…."* This is the solution for the sin-cursed mess of humanity that has been doomed to live without God throughout all generations. A good question asked at this point would be, "What is it that makes this new man new?"

This new quality of humanity, that the Amplified translation of Ephesians 2:15 mentions, is the spiritual condition of man's heart completely transformed by the life and nature of God. At the moment of a man's conversion, eternal life destroys the nature of sin and creates in him a divine nature, just like God himself. Eternal life in us is just as pure and holy as it is in God. Eternal life is not to be over-emphasized as just making it to heaven, it is heaven coming to live in us. **Eternal life is life in the absolute sense.** It is the very life and nature of God himself. It is every bit as powerful in us as it is in God. John 1:3 says, *"In him was life and the life was the light of men."* Acts 3:16 calls Jesus the "Prince of Life" or the "Author of Life." Jesus made it quite clear that this was the reason for his coming. In John 10:10 Jesus said, *"… I have come that you might have life, and have it more abundantly."*

The life and nature of God is what made Jesus different than any other man alive. When Jesus was raised up from the dead it was by the glory of the Father. He was made alive in spirit. It was eternal life that raised him, and it is eternal life that makes us new creatures. God's nature, and everything that it can do, is now the greatest part of us. We are by nature divine children of the One and only great and mighty God. We are heirs of God and joint heirs with Jesus.

In John 3:3 of the Carpenters Translation, Jesus said, *"I want to make it clear, that no one can be a member of God's family unless he is fathered from above.'"* In the Wade Translation, *"...unless a man is begotten from above, he can have no experience of the dominion of God."*

This brings us right back to the original plan. God made man in his own image and likeness. He desired, at the beginning, to have a family without spot or wrinkle. The heart of man, once again, can experience that pure and holy love of

God. At the "new birth," man is made in the image and likeness of God again. God is **now** his Father. Dominion is **now** restored to man, to whom it was originally given. It is the life and nature of God which represents divine authority. God has a family and man has the assignment to share these truths with the world, so the family can grow.

The life of the believer is now as perfectly authoritative as God himself. We have nothing to be ashamed of, or condemned about, ever again. Sin can no longer hold us captive. Every work of Satan is made of **no effect** through the "triumph" of our Lord Jesus Christ. All of this dominion comes to us as a result of the inner change that took place at the point of justification. The Amplified translation of Ephesians 2:5 says, *"He gave us the very life of Christ Himself, the same new life with which he quickened Him."* All limits are removed.

We can literally do all things through Christ who gives us strength. The spirit world is at our beck and call.

God has made it that way for His "born again" man; complete authority on the earth to fulfill God's plan. A plan that includes all men everywhere.

Have you ever wondered why the Bible is so optimistic about YOU and your future? Have you ever questioned the absoluteness of scriptures that sound too good to be true? For instance, the scripture quoted earlier, Romans 8:17, "*...more than conquerors,*" or 2 Corinthians 2:14, "*...always leads us in triumph in Christ*" (NKJV). When Paul tells us that we can do all things through Christ who strengthens us, and that we are strong in the Lord and in the power of His Might, he is encouraging us to assume our position in the "finished work of Christ." We will never again have to strive for victory! We own the victory; it came with our salvation and, might I add, through a great price.

Everything that Jesus conquered was for us. Every "ounce" of his victory was set to our account as though we did it ourselves. His "massive" triumph over death, hell, and the grave is as though we were there and we defeated the devil ourselves. Satan is no threat! He is a defeated foe and an eternal loser.

We are seated with Christ, where we govern in the eternities, as sons of God. The spiritual realm is the place where we have the privilege of exercising our authority. God has made us *co-laborers* in the spirit world. This is where our seat of authority is. We are not struggling in the earth to gain success; we already have every spiritual blessing in the heavens. The weapons of our warfare are not carnal but mighty through God for effective success. What we joyfully enforce, here in the earth, is already an established fact in the eternities. Our victory is real!

Chapter 7
God's Family / New Creatures

Genesis 1:1 says, *"In the beginning, God created the heavens and the earth."* Did you ever wonder how God created? Wouldn't it be awesome to learn how God does what He does?

GOD BEGAN BY PREPARING the earth for the creation of life. He separated the seas and the waters, the sky and the lands. Then he created living things, such as trees and proper vegetation. Now he was ready to fill the earth with creatures. God made fish to swim in the seas, birds to fly in the air, and animals to roam on the land. We don't know how many of each species God made, but we do know that he did desire for each part of His creation to multiply. God's instructions were for each species to reproduce *after its* "own kind." This simply means that dogs were to reproduce dogs and cats were to reproduce cats.

God created everything to have "order" because God Himself exists in order. Even the way God created was accomplished in order. Everything that was created was done so through God the Father, God the Son, and God the Holy Spirit working together as one. With this in mind; isn't it interesting that the third person of the *Trinity*, the Holy Spirit, is mentioned **first** before God the Father or the Son (Genesis 1:2)? When you understand the "divine" order of the *Trinity*, you can see that it makes perfect sense.

God the Father is the *designer* of all things. He draws up the blueprint of the whole world. He has the plan for your life and mine. God's plans are good for each of us and we gain so much when we understand and obey the Father's will.

If the Father has the plan for the world, then he needs someone to carry out the plan. This is the work of God the Son. He, Jesus, is the *initiator* of God's plan. He speaks and acts out the script or blueprint. If you think about it, when you give action to something, the mind plays an important role in the attitude by which the action is done. However, actions are expressed in only two ways. One either speaks a thought with their voice or they express a thought with their body through gestures. Jesus was the perfect "divine" expression of his Father on the earth. Jesus said more than once that he spoke only what the Father said to him and did only those things that he saw the Father do. This is the how we can conclude that it is Jesus who says, "Light be" in Genesis 1:3.

This is how we as God's children begin to establish our place in him. It is our "action of faith" that will produce results. Letting your *words and* actions agree is a "key element" *in experiencing God's plan for your life*. We must learn to express the thoughts of Jesus through both words *and* actions. Colossians 3:17 says, *"And whatever you **do**, whether **in word or deed**, do it all in the name of the Lord Jesus, giving thanks to God the*

Father through him." Daniel 32:11 says that those who know God will be confident and do exploits. A lifestyle of doing great exploits for God comes from a healthy understanding of our place in God. To know God means to experience him, which will produce great boldness to act.

Now we come to Genesis 1:2 where the Holy Spirit is mentioned first before the Father and the Son. This must have been significant in the creation process. As we can see, the Holy Spirit was "hovering over the water." The word *hover* means to incubate. Just as an egg is warmed in an incubation process, the Holy Spirit was warming up the very place where God the Father envisioned creation.

The significance to this thought is quite relevant to our lives as well. We need to realize that the same way the Father interacted with the Son and the Holy Spirit, in perfect harmony, is exactly the same he desires to commune with us. Everything pertaining to our success

in life can be found through our relationship with God and his written Word. Jesus said, "...*if you abide in me and my
words abide in you, you will ask what
you desire and it will be done for
you*" (John 15:7). So, whether you hear
God's precise word to your heart or live
out of the Holy Scriptures, success is
guaranteed.

The reason that the Holy Spirit's
action upon the face of the deep is so
important is that it reveals his omniscient
mind. God is all-knowing. The Holy Spirit
shows us the preliminary work that is
done for the miraculous to manifest. God
wanted us to know that the Holy Spirit
will always be in position **ahead** of time
to prepare the way for your faith. If what
you express are the thoughts of God, either by the voice of God to your heart or
by the written word of God, you can be
confident that the Holy Spirit is already
engaged in anticipation of your miracle.
God wants us to see his "pattern."

It is extremely important to God
that his views be revealed to us. God

wants you to know how important it is to have results. Everything God said in creation **appeared.** God didn't create anything that took time to be fulfilled. When he said, "Light be," it was. **God expected it to happen.** He never even thought for a moment that it might not happen. This was and is normal for God. Genesis 1:4 says, *"...that God saw what He created and said it was good."* Notice that God took time to inspect what he had made. Remember, this is God's attitude revealed to us about what he creates.

The whole idea of a "manifestation" comes from God. He is the great *inspector* over every project. His quality control is flawless. He will not accept anything that is not perfect. The only way to receive the approval of **good** is to be the "exact image" of his intention. *Light* was exactly as it was intended, and so was the rest of creation. In fact, when everything was completed, God inspected it once more and stamped it, "very good!"

As you can see God's attitude about creation sets up or initiates the entire revelation for the redemption of man. From the Old Testament men and women of God to the New Testament believer, supernatural results will dominate the mysticism of what we believe. Without them we have a "nice" religion but lack the proof of our relationship to God. Never in Jesus' earth walk do we see him nervous or fretful that the will of God might **not** manifest. Jesus was always bold and filled with the spirit of dominion. He knew that the Holy Spirit was the *direct pathway* to the miracle he needed. He never questioned the Holy Spirit's willingness to perform or his faithfulness to complete the work started. What an awesome position Jesus had—sandwiched in between the authenticity of God the Father and the surety of the Holy Spirit. The Father has never failed to produce a plan that worked, and the Holy Spirit has never failed to manifest a plan that was courageously acted on.

How would your life be affected if you took advantage of the way that God creates? If you were certain that your interaction with God made it impossible for your prayers to fail, how would that make you feel? What if you knew with absolute certainty that the Holy Spirit would never miss the opportunity to produce results for you? How would you act then? It is paramount that we as believers practice being assertive and bold concerning our relationship with God. It's time that we all start to act like we are sure of the way God works!

Chapter 8
"The works I do, you will do also."

AS CHRIST'S REPRESENTATIVES we have his authority. As you can imagine, "backbone" is necessary to work the works of our Lord. So, there is no better place to acquire this backbone than in our identity with Jesus, our Lord.

I believe that your heart confirms the truth that you are not limited by the many doctrines of the world that teach your success is based upon works. No, thank God the finished work of Jesus was a complete work! We have the easy part of responding to it. Our qualification is in Jesus. Everything he did for us was more than enough to secure our success and complete victory.

Have you ever been in a situation where you desired to bless someone financially, yet you didn't have the money to do so? I think we have all been there. How frustrating it is when you want to

help someone but don't have the resources to do so. On the other hand, if
the resources were plenteous, or even
just enough, then you could give it away.
James commented on this;

*"If a brother or sister is naked and desti-
tute of daily food, and one of you says to
them, 'Depart in peace, be warmed and
filled,' but you do not give them the
things which are needed for the body,
what does it profit? Thus also faith by itself, if it does not have works, is dead"*
James 2:15-17 (NKJV).

If God requires us to give what we
have to others when there is a need,
then we can rely upon God who has supplied us with his strength to work with us
to fulfill our needs. This is the reason
why God has given us all things to enjoy.
We are fully equipped to run and finish
our race.

We, as believers, ought to desire to
be a blessing to anyone we meet. The
world is in such need that there are nu-
merous opportunities available to those

who desire to help others. After teaching some of the truths in this book at a certain church, the pastor of the church stood up before the congregation and shared a testimony. He said, "I was in a place of business and I overheard a man talking with a woman about his difficulties. He told of the chronic pain that he lived with, [pain that ran] down his back and into his leg. He explained how, for some time, he had been seeking help from medical professionals. In his disappointment [the man] explained that nothing they did helped. Then he made a statement which was the perfect lead in, 'I just need someone to help me.'" The pastor then confessed to his congregation. "I stood there and did nothing, but after what I've learned here tonight, I will never do nothing again."

All through the Bible, whenever a man or woman **knew** that they possessed the power of God and could use it to bring benefit to themselves or others, they had miracles. Jesus waited until he was anointed with the Holy Ghost and "power" from his baptism in the river

Jordan to venture out in ministry. In fact, one of the platforms of Jesus' teaching ministry is found in Luke 4:18-19 (NKJV),

"The Spirit of the LORD is upon Me, Because He has anointed Me To preach the gospel to the poor; He has sent Me to heal the brokenhearted, To proclaim liberty to the captives And recovery of sight to the blind, To set at liberty those who are oppressed; To proclaim the acceptable year of the LORD.'"

Why would Jesus have to tell folks that He was anointed? Couldn't the people **see** that the "anointing" was upon Him? Well, the results He produced were **evidence**, but they couldn't see the anointing. So even in the ministry of Jesus people had to believe in the unseen.

Jesus, of course, had developed his spiritual senses through his relationship with his Father until the unseen was extremely real at all times. As Jesus walked through a crowd one day, unbeknown to Him, a woman who had a serious medical condition reached out and touched Him. This woman had suffered for twelve years with blood loss and would most likely die soon. When she touched Jesus, actually just the hem of His garment, she felt the tangible power of God go into her body and heal her of that condition. Interestingly enough, Jesus also knew that power had been released from him. This caused a commotion, as Jesus sought out the woman and her story was revealed.

Early in my ministry I traveled with Rev. Kenneth E. Hagin, and ministered with him as a member of the Rhema Singers and Band. I remember at one particular *Campmeeting,* as Rev. Hagin was at the pulpit teaching, the anointing became increasingly strong on him. In fact, I ran and stood behind him to steady him and keep him from falling. He told the people in the congregation that he was unable to come to the main floor to minister because the anointing had settled in his legs and he couldn't walk well. Whenever this happened, Rev. Hagin would have two members from the singers and band minister for him.

He called the first team member, Anne, to the pulpit and laid his hands on hers. Then he instructed her to minister the anointing he had placed in her hands to the people, in the Name of Jesus. Then he quickly turned around to look for Dean, the drummer. When Rev. Hagin did this, he was somewhat startled because he didn't know that I was right behind him. We ended up face to face. He jumped and uttered a noise, and so did I. I quickly moved to one side, trying to avoid him, and, strangely enough, he moved to the same side. Once again, I ended up right in front of him, I moved the other way, and so did he. This time he grunted to show his frustration. He straightened up, looked at me and said, "Oh, alright, you'll do!" Everyone laughed, including me. He said, "Stretch out your hands," which I did, and then he placed his hands in mine. He said, "I transfer this anointing into your hands; now go and minister it to the people, in the Name of Jesus."

As I headed toward the people, the power of God began pulsating in my hands. I could literally "feel" this power. The closer I came to the people the stronger it became, and it began to surround my hands like a glove.

The first person I laid my hands on immediately received, as that power came out of my hands. It was very easy to release the power because I could feel it so strong. In other words, because I was very confident that it was there, it made sense to me that I could release it. Many healings happened that night. I was a believer in the *tangible* power of God.

Many years later I was asked to teach and minister at the Prayer and Healing school at Kenneth Hagin Ministries. I remember, during the first three years, that the power of God would come many times as a tangible force. It was easy to minister the power to the people when I could feel the anointing. Just knowing it was tangibly there made releasing it very natural. It doesn't take much faith when your senses are in agreement with the spiritual truth you are acting on. I remember Rev. Hagin saying that when the power of God is tangible, more people are healed. You can see why it becomes easier for people to receive when they can physically detect the anointing. You can also see how dull we have become spiritually, when we have to rely on our physical senses to believe God.

After those first three years, the tangible power of God just vanished. I asked the Lord one day, out of desperation, "Where did you go? What did I do to offend you?" Truthfully, I wasn't ready for His reply. The Lord said, "For the past three years you have released the power because you felt it, now it's time to release it by faith." The awesome thing about the next five years is that I witnessed an increase in results by double, triple, and even quadruple. The reason why? I didn't have to rely on **a feeling.** I could minister the anointing whenever the need arose, and with great confidence, because the Word said I was anointed and, if I believed, the power would flow. And it did!

Elisha is a great example of this. Back in the day when Elisha was the prodigy of Elijah, Elijah tested the commitment of Elisha. Elisha had asked Elijah for a "double portion" of the anointing that was on his life. Elijah told Elisha that the anointing would only be transferred if he **saw** him when God came to take him to heaven. Elijah tested Elisha's faithfulness. He tried many times to get him to leave his side, but each time Elisha would say, "As surely as my soul lives, I will not leave you." One day they came to the river Jordan and Elijah took hold of his "mantle," which represented the anointing, and struck the river. It parted, and the two men crossed over on dry ground. That day Elijah was taken in a whirlwind to heaven. As the event took place, Elisha was there to witness everything. With Elijah gone, the mantle fell to the ground, and Elisha went over and picked it up.

I think it is interesting that Elisha didn't **feel** anything. He actually had to test it to make sure that the anointing was in the mantle. It is like test driving a car, you want to make sure that it works well before you invest your money into it. There was no sense in Elisha starting a miracle ministry if he did not have the "power" to produce miracles. He struck the river Jordan with the mantle and he said, "Where is the God of Elijah?" The water split in the same way it had for Elijah. This was the convincing evidence that God was in the mantle whether it felt like it or not. So that means that the many miracles Elisha performed, were most likely based on what Elisha learned at the river Jordan. He learned that he had the "power."

Come on now, you can't give something you don't have. But when you have it, that's another story; now you can give it away. Elisha became so confident in the power of God, that God assisted Elisha when he initiated the work in the same way that Elisha assisted God when he initiated the work. There were times when the word of the Lord came to Elisha with specific directions. As Elisha obeyed, miracles were experienced. Other times, Elisha would give a command even when he didn't have a word from the Lord. As the people obeyed the command of Elisha, the miracle would happen just as it did when he had the word of the Lord. Do you see what Elisha learned? Whether God speaks to you, which is heaven moving on your behalf, or you become so confident in the presence of God that you initiate the miracle, which is you working on heaven's behalf, it happens. Either way, the more you recognize your authority in the realm of the spirit, the easier it is to confidently release your faith.

I remember a time that I was asked to take a prayer cloth to Rev. Hagin, to have him pray over it. After a brief time visiting with him, I asked him to pray. Instead of handing him the cloth, I held it in my hand so he would have to put his hand over mine to pray. I specifically wanted to know **when** the

power of God left his hand. He began by
thanking God for the covenant we have
through the Lord. He then reminded the
Lord that healing was the children's
bread. I felt nothing. Then he said, "And
now Father, thank you for the anointing
that you have anointed me with." When
he said that, like a "starburst," the presence of God left his hand and went into
the cloth. It also **hit** my hand! I felt it as
real as anything I've ever felt. The more
he reminded the Lord, about that anointing, the stronger that starburst became
until it spread out from my hand and began going up my arm. This is what I
learned; when he talked about the
anointing that the Lord had anointed him
with, he was remembering the vision he
had in 1950. In this vision, he was taken
up into heaven and stood before the
Lord. At this time, the Lord asked him to
stretch out his hands, and as he did, the
Lord placed his finger into each of them.
The power of God began to burn in Rev.
Hagin's hands. For the twenty years I
knew him, whenever he told that story,
God's power would become tangible. As
he remembered the spiritual experience

that happened years ago, it became just as real to him, over and over again. The more real the anointing becomes to you, the easier it is to release it by faith.

This is the reason that Jesus and men, like the Old Testament prophets, continued in the anointing without question. They all accepted the fact that they had the anointing to use. All of them learned to be confident with the anointing of God; we can see the benefits of that confidence.

The disciples were also a unique group of followers of our Lord that revealed the heart of the ministry of God's presence. They carried on the ministry of Jesus with great success. The common denominator of their success was their confidence that they possessed the power to do the works.

If we were to look at Peter and John, we very clearly see this principle. Acts 3:1-9 NKJV says, *"Now Peter and John went up together to the temple at the hour of prayer, the ninth hour. And a certain man lame from his mother's womb was carried, whom they laid daily at the gate of the temple which is called Beautiful, to ask alms from those who entered the temple; who, seeing Peter and John about to go into the temple, asked for alms. And fixing his eyes on him, with John, Peter said, "Look at us." So he gave them his attention, expecting to receive something from them. Then Peter said, "Silver and gold I do not have, but what I do have I give you: In the name of Jesus Christ of Nazareth, rise up and walk." And he took him by the right hand and lifted him up, and immediately his feet and ankle bones received strength. So he, leaping up, stood and walked and entered the temple with them—walking, leaping, and praising God. And all the people saw him walking and praising God."*

Notice the boldness of Peter and John as they told the beggar to look at them. Of course he is going to expect to receive something. What really gives someone the right to lead another to this kind of expectation? Peter tells you why he was so confident and why he was so demonstrative. Peter said, "What I have, I give you." Where did Peter get the power of God that made this man well? And what made him so sure that it would work?

It's clear to see that God will work with you when you are confident to act as though you have something to give. Jesus emphasized this to His disciples in Matthew 10:1, 7-8 (NKJV),

1 "And when He had called His twelve disciples to Him, He gave them power over unclean spirits, to cast them out, and to heal all kinds of sickness and all kinds of disease."

7-8 "And as you go, preach(with this power), saying, 'The kingdom of heaven is at hand.' Heal the sick with this power), cleanse the lepers (with this power), raise the dead (with this power), cast out demons(with this power). Freely you have received(this power), freely give(this power)."

The *key* to this passage is that Jesus was a tremendous example of flawless results while doing the Father God's work on earth. Because of his success in the anointing, he clearly portrayed the heart of his father with unparalleled results. The disciples were unaware that the power of God on Jesus would do anything but succeed.

For example, if I could buy a gumball from a machine for a dime, I would expect to receive one gumball for every dime I put into the machine. If I took one hundred dimes and placed them into the gumball machine, one at a time, I could expect to receive one hundred gumballs. If my children witnessed this experience, what would they think if I gave each of them one hundred dimes? Of course, they would be excited to get one hundred gumballs. Now, let's look at the mindset of the disciples in light of this example. If they were given the same power, or anointing, that Jesus used to cast out devils and heal the sick, they would be completely satisfied that the **same power** would, indeed, produce the same results. Jesus said, "Freely you have received, freely give." Do you notice here that Jesus doesn't require any other prerequisites for success? He simply says, now that you have it, give it away. In the minds of the disciples there was no question that they would have success. The same confidence that Peter had when he walked with Jesus was now embedded in his heart because of the presence of the Holy Spirit.

So how can we apply this to our world? How can we produce the same results? The Bible is a book of facts. It is a "bookie's" dream come true! It tells you what you can expect before you step out to believe God. It is the ultimate book of future expectations. In the same way as described earlier, with Jesus and His disciples, confidence is greatest when you are **sure** you will succeed.

The mind of man will fret over the possibility of failure. When you understand who you are and your place in the covenant Jesus secured for you, and as you become aware of the power of God which is the ultimate ability to bring change, the chance that you will act on God's word is great. Remember, *"Faith is betting your life on the unseen realities of God."* And these **unseen realities** are what you must give complete allegiance to.

God has given you an imagination which allows you to see the unseen, feel the intangible, and believe in the impossible. If your mind can't see it, mark it down—it won't happen. Envision the power of God in you and upon you. See God with great power flowing out of you and into the problem, wherever it may be. If you believe you have the anointing, then **act like it!** Your *faith* is the substance of things imagined or hoped for. When you hear a good testimony or see a person work the works of God, you gain a mental picture, and belief, that God could also work with you. You can release the power of God. It belongs to you; **release it with your words or actions because you can!**

Jesus decreed in Mark 16:15-20 (NKJV),

"Go into all the world and preach the gospel to every creature. He who believes and is baptized will be saved; but he who does not believe will be condemned. And these signs will follow those who believe: In My name they will cast out demons; they will speak with new tongues; they will take up serpents; and if they drink anything deadly, it will by no means hurt them; they will lay hands on the sick, and they will recover." So then, after the Lord had spoken to them, He was received up into heaven, and sat down at the right hand of God. And they went out and preached everywhere, the Lord working with them and confirming the word through the accompanying signs. Amen."

Jesus specified these works so that we would not be left guessing about our role. Anyone can go through the motions of laying hands on the sick or casting out devils. However, if you want it to work, you better **know** God and His power. This is why it is so important for you to understand the significance of "knowing" that you are anointed.

A while back, I ministered in a healing school for a period of ten years. It was the perfect environment to experiment with the anointing. I would try different ways of using the anointing to see if there were results. I wanted to discover the properties of God's power for myself. How I worked with the sick, or how I worked with my helpers in healing school to produce results varied as I was made more aware of the anointing. I discovered that the stronger my association was with "who I was in Christ," the more effective I was with the anointing. In other words, the more "real" God was to me, the easier it was to produce results. I trust that you are **hearing** again and again how very IMPORTANT it is that we open our hearts to the "tangibility" of God.

The seven *Sons of Sceva* wished they had a relationship with God! Luke records, in Acts 19, that there were seven sons of Sceva who were Jewish exor-

cists. They had witnessed the ex-
traordinary miracles the apostle Paul did,
so they took it upon themselves to speak
to a demon spirit "in the name of Jesus
whom Paul preaches." The evil spirit responded, "Jesus I know, and Paul I know,
but who are you?" Then the evil spirit,
empowering the man whom it was in,
overtook the exorcists and beat them.
Notice, the demon didn't know those who
were unaware of the significance of the
Name. Or you could say, if you don't
know who YOU are in relation to Jesus
then the devil does not have to obey
you. The devil knew Jesus and Paul because they knew who they were in God,
and they knew that the devil could not
resist them in the power of the Spirit. Do
you see how important it is to understand YOUR position in God's family and
your authority in the earth?

I can remember, on certain occa-
sions, the Spirit of the Lord showing me
different methods of working with the
anointing. He would encourage me to
"expect" that he would do something
right then, in the service. In those days,

no one really saw healings, they just preached about them.

At first, when I had these experiences, he taught me **to believe that he would do** something, NOW. And he did, as long as I acted boldly. Next, he taught me **to believe that I could do** something right now. And I did, and the miracle happened! Then he taught me **to believe in the power**, whether or not I could feel it. This completely changed everything, because I was no longer limited to a feeling to believe and experience God.

Now things became interesting! When you don't feel anything, how can you be bold? How can you tell people to "expect" to see change and declare that they will receive right then? Well, you must believe it yourself. I discovered that the stronger my conviction became, the more healings we had; it became difficult to distinguish whether I was working with Him or He was working with me. This is our goal; to be "inseparable" with the Lord, one in thought, word and action. And one in results!

Truthfully, when we TAKE God's word at face value, a man or woman who will simply act, even if they are inspired because of "intestinal fortitude," will get some results. Let's not shoot at the target aimlessly, not being sure how many "bulls-eyes" we'll get. Let's be confident and courageous, shooting with accuracy and expertise. There is no more time for hoping and praying. God sent Jesus to secure, for the human race, the honor of becoming sons and daughters of God. Peter said that we are a "special people", a royal priesthood, a holy nation. Each human being to accept Jesus will become "one single spirit with him." According to Paul, we are "new creatures" in Christ. No longer outcasts, wandering *around* without knowledge. We are **sons** and we know it. We are filled with the same Spirit and anointing as Jesus, and we are fully aware of him. We are invested with the authority that comes from the throne of God, and we are poised to use it effectively, on purpose, to accomplish the

mission of "revealing" Jesus to the world.
"Freely you have received, now, freely
give" (Matt.10:8).

Chapter 9
Knowing Him

THUS FAR WE HAVE PRESENTED the revelation of *who you are,* so you can identify the reality of your own life.

Seeing things like God sees them is the "beginning" of many wonderful years of experiencing God's best. A revelation of God will make you a danger to the enemy. You now know how to separate the truth from the lie or the spirit from the flesh. Jeremiah best describes this thought,

"Thus says the Lord: Let not the wise and skillful person glory and boast in his wisdom and skill; let not the mighty and powerful person glory and boast in his strength and power; let not the person who is rich [in physical gratification and earthly wealth] glory and boast in his [temporal satisfactions and earthly] riches; But let him who glories glory in this: that he understands and knows Me [personally and practically, directly discern-

ing and recognizing My character], that I am the Lord, Who practices loving-kindness, judgment, and righteousness in the earth, for in these things I delight, says the Lord"
Jeremiah 9:23-24 (AMPC).

Jesus remarked to his disciples that when we seek first God's kingdom and his righteousness, all the things of life will be added to us. Jesus should know, he stayed continually aware of his Father through fellowship and by speaking of him, and revealing him to all. When we consider the relationship that Jesus had with his Father, you will see that his reliance upon the Father, for everything he did and said on the earth, was paramount. So Jesus explained,
"I tell you the truth, the Son can do nothing by himself. He does only what he sees the Father doing. Whatever the Father does, the Son also does. For the Father loves the Son and shows him everything he is doing. In fact, the Father will show him how to do even greater works than healing this man. Then you will truly be astonished" John 5:19-20 (NLT).

Contrary to the opinion of the religious, Jesus developed in his relationship with the Father God and his understanding of the spirit world. There was a progression involved as Jesus grew in awareness and authority. We find that as a young boy Jesus had already become enlightened to his identity and accepted enough of his place, as the Son of God, that he began to challenge the spiritual skeptics of the day. As he grew in wisdom and in the favor of God, a spiritual maturity developed in him that shaped the decisions of his life.

40 "And the child grew and waxed strong [in spirit], filled with wisdom, and God's grace was upon him" Luke 2:40.

As we look further in the same passage, from verses 41-52, you find Jesus alone for three days, at the age of twelve, reasoning with the Pharisees in the temple. Jesus, I am sure, didn't plan this; it just became the most natural thing his soul could do. The things of God were so important and real to Jesus that having a discussion about his father was the most exciting thing he could have imagined at his age.

When his parents took him to Jerusalem, and to the temple, his many emotions and thoughts, combined with the internal destiny that spoke through his soul, came together and most likely overwhelmed this twelve-year-old boy. I don't believe Jesus even considered that he should **not** be doing this. He wasn't a negative thinker. Everything about being in the synagogue and hearing men debate the scriptures was the paramount reality of his life, thus far.

Can you imagine how many times Jesus had an "unction" from the Spirit of God about his purpose and destiny? The Holy Ghost is the Spirit of Truth that will lead us into **all truth**. *Truth* means reality. So, the job of the Holy Spirit is to lead us into the realities of God; those places in the spirit where all things make sense. Places where *what and who* you are become real enough that the earthly world, for a moment, becomes dull and insignificant. Why else would a twelve-year-old boy spend three days in the synagogue reasoning with grownups; very much unaware of time and his responsibilities to his earthly parents?

As a parent I can relate to this. I remember when my daughters were young; they would be content until they needed something. When that need became important enough to them, then they were interested in knowing where their parents were.

If Jesus became so aware of spiritual things that it brought him comfort and peace without concern; then we too can develop a sensitivity to everything in God that pertains to our lives and our relationship with God.

Isn't it interesting that not one need of Jesus was mentioned for those three days? Who took care of him, where did he eat, and what about sleep, and safety? We miss out on so much by being too earthly minded.

Jesus was in the temple at age twelve, demonstrating an amazing understanding of the scriptures. The next time we see him, is eighteen years later, at thirty years old. He is ready to enter into his ministry; having been baptized in the river Jordan by John the Baptist. What do you suppose he did during those unrecorded teenage and young adult years?

I believe that during those unrecorded years, Jesus must have continued to show the same commitment he showed at twelve years old. We know from Paul's writings in Hebrews 11:6, *"without faith it is impossible to please Him, for he who comes to God must believe that He is and He rewards those who diligently seek Him."* It would take a consistency of meditation and prayer to gain such understanding of the spirit realm. If you will remember, Jesus was a carpenter by trade. So, it's not like he sat around all day in meditation. He had to pursue this relationship just like we do. However, you need to know that spiritual things are not like earthly things.

You can progress very quickly because of the help of the Holy Spirit. It is religion that has done us such a disservice by inferring that we must work for the grace that Jesus alone has provided. Religion "paints" the picture of a godly relationship as serving the church; being a part of a group and serving others rather than developing a personal connection with God.

There is no higher understanding than this; that God is very tangible and we, as spirit beings, can know and experience him continually. Jesus said in John 10:15, *"I know the Father, even as He knows me."* I have often pondered that statement because of its profound depth. Think about it. Could it be possible for a man to know God even as God knows the man? This seems preposterous, doesn't it? However, if you read it as, "I experience the Father even as the Father experiences me," then it becomes attainable. When we meet with God, our experience with him should be just as real as his experience is with us. This is why I emphasize that any Christian can go very far with Jesus in a very short time. One experience with Jesus will make you hunger for many more. "Oh, taste and see, that the Lord is good".

If we will remember, in the gospels, Jesus would often arise early to go to a solitary place to pray and spend time with the Father. We have learned, in the earthly realm, that the more time you spend with someone, the more thoroughly you know them. We see Jesus on the Mount of Transfiguration in fellowship with his Father. The glory of God within him radiated out of His clothes and face. The "glory cloud" was present; Moses and Elijah were present and God the Father spoke audibly. Not bad for a night in prayer! What if this was not the **only time** Jesus had a spiritual experience like this? We have a record of this event because he took his disciples with him. What about all those times that he went alone?

My questions are meant to open your mind to the possibilities that lie hidden inside the walls of traditionalism and

religion. Why don't we know or experience God in this way as well?

*"Most assuredly, I say to you, We speak
what We know and testify what We have
seen, and you do not receive Our witness. If I have told you earthly things
and you do not believe, how will you believe if I tell you heavenly things? No one
has ascended to heaven but He who
came down from heaven, that is, the Son
of Man who is in heaven"* John 3:11-13
(NKJV).

    Jesus is giving us tremendous keys
to enter into a spiritual awareness of
heavenly things. He is talking about being in two places at the same time. The
secret to the success of Jesus on the
earth was that while he walked in this
world, he lived out of the spiritual world.
Jesus had great confidence in the things
from above. He "bet his life on the unseen realities" of His Father God. He was
"astonished" that Nicodemus, a spiritual
leader, didn't know these heavenly
things; God the Father, the power of the

Holy Ghost, and angels were all very real to Jesus.

Realizing, of course, that solitude is so important to our development, and it is also possible that we can continue to develop our spiritual awareness while going about the course of our day? To say NO would bring limitations to the truth that God is everywhere at all times. If we are not finding him all day long then we are not applying ourselves. Please remember that the effort required for a relationship with God was accomplished through the effort of Jesus in his life, death, and resurrection. Jesus never presents the idea that connecting with God from your heart is odd or difficult. He does, however, reveal how contrary the world, the flesh and religion are and can be to you. So enjoying and interacting with spiritual things is to your spirit the most natural and normal thing you could encounter. Can you make the effort to devalue, minimize, and consider unimportant the things of the world and the flesh that you encounter every day?

To do so would free up your attention and focus to consider God!

The apostle Paul added his thoughts to this subject as he told the church at Corinth because of the tremendous adversities that came against him they should learn how to keep their eyes on things that are unseen. He mentioned that to look at the "seen" realm which is always changing would bring no profit to one's life. Doesn't it seem interesting to you that we are instructed to look at something that we cannot see? How is this possible?

In John 4:24 Jesus says, "God is Spirit, and those who worship Him must worship in spirit and truth." Since we are spirit beings then we qualify to worship God. If this is true and it is, then it should not be as difficult as we might have thought to develop a wonderful prayer life where we come to **know God the Father as He knows us.**

He developed his awareness to this realm by continually acknowledging it.

The time Jesus spent with His Father made him very sure of his place in the miraculous. Jesus is the greatest example of a man becoming so proficient in accessing the spiritual realm, that using heavenly power and glory to conquer earthly troubles was effortless.

Paul comments in 2 Corinthians 5:6-8 NKJV, *"So we are always confident, knowing that while we are at home in the body we are absent from the Lord. For we walk by faith, not by sight. We are confident, yes, well pleased rather to be absent from the body and to be present with the Lord."*

This is a teeter totter principle. The more aware of the body and the world we are, the less aware of the Lord we will be. So to automatically increase our spirituality we turn our back on the world while turning our face toward God. Isn't this the practice of fasting and prayer? Jesus gave this practice to the disciples when they were unable to cast a demon out of a boy, in Mark chapter 9. The part that prayer and fasting plays is to sensitize you to spiritual things by laying aside earthly things. Living a fasted lifestyle is so much more than not eating a meal. It is continually staying sharp and aware of God by lessening the importance of the flesh and the world.

I remember what the practice schedule was like, during the years I played high school and college football. At the beginning of the season, we had three practices a day. This meant that we started the morning with a two-and-a-half-hour practice, followed up by another of the same in the afternoon. If that wasn't enough, many times we gathered for films in the evening. The reason for all of this was to "saturate" our minds with each play and our individual responsibilities. The coaches knew that if we were working so hard to remember the plays we wouldn't be responding naturally. There was no time in the heat of battle to try and remember what we should do. Our focus at that point should be nothing but all-out effort.

Right in the midst of the world and its chaos, when the flesh is talking the loudest, you can place your confidence in the reality of God's presence within you. This will persuade you to bet your life on him. Life really can be lived with that much confidence and authority. God has more than abundantly supplied us with proof after proof to convince us of His love and faithfulness.

Have you ever heard the expression, "The lights are on, but no one is home"? We use this saying to describe someone who is not paying attention, they are day dreaming or just not engaged in what is happening or being spoken at the time. When we worship God, we are simply making the choice to honor the spiritual connection that we have with God.

Jesus said that we must worship in spirit and in truth. To do this you must approach God with nothing but the simplicity of who you are. As Paul said in Hebrews 5:14-16, ..."with practice, even your senses can be exercised to discern both good and evil." Jesus spent time practicing what was real from His heart. This is worshipping God!!! Look at what Jesus said in Matthew 6:5-6 (MSG), *"And when you come before God, don't turn that into a theatrical production either. All these people making a regular show out of their prayers, hoping for stardom! Do you think God sits in a box seat? Here's what I want you to do: Find a quiet, secluded place so you won't be tempted to role-play before God. Just be there as simply and honestly as you can manage.* **The focus will shift from you to God, and you will begin to sense his grace.**"

As you can imagine, when you are free from whatever distracts you, you will be more effective in engaging your spirit. Your ability to concentrate on the unseen realm is easier when there is solitude. I'm sure you will experience this truth, if you will practice worshipping God in the quiet times. It will be easier to hear God and engage your spirit even when things are busy. The busier things get and the more complicated our society becomes, the harder it is to find time to spend with God.

If we will adjust our perspective of how we view a relationship with God, we will naturally have greater experiences. Think for a moment about Adam and Eve. Even after they had sinned, they continued to hear the sound of God's voice in complete sentences and recognized His presence. This only proves that the possibility of being in tune with God as his born again children is so much greater. If Adam and Eve were in tune with God as sinners, then we certainly can become fine tuned with God's voice and presence as sons of God.

So, let's make the adjustment!! See yourself how God sees you. He made you perfectly connected to himself through Christ. Make a concentrated effort to separate the spiritual world from the earthly world. Know in your heart that you do know God and remember that connecting with him is normal. Seeing him everywhere and sensing his amazing presence is your new life. If Jesus did

this in his humanity, then so can we.
Sure, there are many distractions, but
just as sure, the grace of God is greater.
"Greater is He that is in you, than he
that is in the world".

SUMMARY

IN EVERY GENERATION, "those who can't, teach, and those who can, do". God has called us to be doers of His word and imitators of the life and ministry of Jesus Christ. At no point were we to question the authenticity of God and His integrity. Man was made by God to most naturally correspond to everything that emanated from God.

The world has lost sight of its purpose. Therefore, the *identity crisis* speaks every day and all day long. If you listen to it. This *identity crisis* is revealed in every kind of evil intention of man's heart. Every despicable act proves that this crisis exists. When patterns are set and generations are born without a biblical blueprint, the spiral downward is quicker than imagined.

It's time to stop the cycle! To those who are satisfied, raising the "bar" for a quality connection to God may seem like a rebellion or revolt. If the

Identity of Christ handed down through the shed blood on the cross is to be acknowledged, a group of followers must supersede the qualifications of mediocrity and rise to meet the mind of God. Only in your proper place, will you see yourself in the glory of his light.

Identity Crisis has taken up the challenge to shine upon you, with simplicity, the predestined plan of the Ancient of Days. If you know him, then you have what he has, you can do what he does, and the authority to grow and develop as he is right now is innately placed within your heart. With only a little determination, exactly like Jesus said in his parable of the tiny mustard seed, faith will ignite the dead wood of formalism. The voice of the Lord is calling for someone to step out from the shadows and yield to the mighty Holy Spirit with enough purpose that the world will know that Jesus is Lord.

The pattern has been patented for years. There is nothing else for God to do. What do you have to lose? If anything in this life means that much to you, then mark it down, you will never operate in the anointing. No man will win if he protects the thing he is afraid to lose. However, if you take to heart the words you have read, then you will no longer fear losing. It is not an option. **Jesus won; therefore, you have won, and you will never stop winning.** You know who you are, what you have, and you are now ready to release the anointing on purpose.

To those who are ready to remove the blinders of religion and with an open heart be challenged to accept the great commission to preach the gospel, your life has just begun…..THE WORKS I DO, YOU SHALL DO ALSO.

ABOUT THE AUTHOR

JIM Hockaday was born again at four years of age. Experiencing the call of God at this time and the desire to preach, Jim led many to the Lord during his childhood. After graduation from Wheaton College in 1983, he traveled with several Christian music groups, including the Spurlows, Truth, and the Living Word Singers.

When God put in Jim's heart a strong desire to know more of Him, he attended Rhema Bible Training Center and graduated in 1988. Immediately following graduation, he joined the Rhema Singers and Band and traveled extensively with Rev. Kenneth E. Hagin and the Group for nearly seven years; during the last several years he had the management responsibility of the Group. Jim was the Coordinator of Prayer and Healing School for Kenneth HaginMinistries, completing his tenth year in May 2004. He founded *Jim Hockaday Ministries, Inc*. in 1991, and since then travels and ministers full time in churches at home and abroad.

Jim is the author of several books, one of which is a *best selling* book, "Until I Come." Jim and his wife Erin (a 1991 graduate of Rhema Bible Training Center and member of the Rhema Singers) reside in the Denver, CO area.

BOOKS PUBLISHED

Until I Come

Jesus said, "Until I come, the works I do you shall do, also." Remember: Jesus had a first miracle, the rest is history!

Living In The Miraculous

Why not know where you're going, know how to get there, and know what to expect when you arrive!

Where Does God Fit In?

Stop wondering and start reading...you will discover God's presence and promises to fit into every place...!

The Miraculous Gospel of John With Commentary

As you read the gospel of John expect to receive an impartation from the life and anointing of the Lord Jesus Christ...live in the miraculous!

Miracles Now

Use these nuggets to inspire your faith and then confirm it by praying the suggested prayers...Expect your miracle now!

Identity Crisis

From time to time a standard is set that redefines *truth*. Identity Crisis was written to do just that.